THE SECRETS OF ATTRACTION

Dawn,
who can find
a virtuous woman? Her price
is far above rubies!
Let your virtue
continue to flow and gently
transform so many
lives!
love
Heather
2013

HEATHER REID

THE SECRETS OF ATTRACTION

HOW YOU CAN TURN FRUSTRATION TO FULFILMENT AND 'LIFE IMPRISONMENT' TO LIFELONG INTIMACY IN YOUR RELATIONSHIP

Dolman Scott

This edition of *The Secrets of Attraction: How you can turn frustration to fulfilment and 'life imprisonment' to lifelong intimacy in your relationship* is published by:

Dolman Scott
Benleaze House, East Harptree
Bristol BS40 6AJ

This publication is designed to support you in your relationship, based on biblical principles. If legal or other professional advice is required, the services of a competent professional should be sought.

A CIP catalogue record for this book is available from the British Library.

ISBN 978-1-905553-39-6

To obtain additional copies of this book Please visit:

www.repositionyourlife.com

Thank you.

*To Robert
for uplifting the trajectory of my life*

*And to countless women everywhere
seeking lasting intimacy and mutual
fulfilment in your relationships*

You deserve it!

CONTENTS

FOREWORD

No matter where in the world I go—and I've been to a lot of places—I always notice one thing. The relationships of that society come down to a man and a woman. As I observe people attending church, walking in the mall, going through airports, and at sporting or social events, I see people walking in couples. I assume many (but not all) are married, especially when accompanied by a few children and a stroller.

One-man-one-woman was God's idea. We have been trying to work that out since Adam and Eve and it's been difficult. Today, divorce rates are high and just as high in the church as outside. Yet, even with divorce rates high, people still hold marriage as the highest standard for couples. Some are trying to redefine a couple as being of the same sex, so they can get married. Living together just isn't enough; they want to carry the label "married." I find that interesting.

At any rate, marital pressures allow marriage counselors to do a booming business and bookstores are full of self-help books about marriage, relationships and sex. All that said, you might ask why we need another book on the dynamics of that basic relationship of one-man-one-woman. The answer is simple: we need more books and insight from men and women who are walking out the one-man-one-woman life and doing it successfully.

That's where Heather Reid and her book, *The Secrets of Attraction,* come in.

I have known Heather and her 'man' Robert since 2001. I met them when I visited their church and I have visited there and them regularly since then. One thing you sense by being around Heather and Robert is that they are committed to each other, to make the one-man-one-woman thing work and work well. They obviously love each other, their children and their God. People like Heather have credibility because they have lived what they are writing about.

Heather isn't content, however, just to talk about things like etiquette or family devotions. Heather talks about the good stuff, which is also the hard stuff, and this is intimacy. She does so with candour, humour and transparency. She shares with you what has been effective for her, without coming off as a know-it-all or condescending.

She is an experienced woman who is a happy member of a one-man-one-woman relationship. She wants to see others succeed as she has, because she too understands that at the end of the day, happiness often comes down to the success of that one-man-one-woman relationship.

So read this book, ladies, and apply the lessons liberally. Men, you can read it too, but not so you can tell your 'woman' what to do, but to learn what you can do to promote and further intimacy with your one-woman.

Thank you, Heather and Robert, for putting your life on display for others who are in a one-man-one-woman life. Thank you for your vulnerability and openness. I pray that your relationship will continually grow stronger and that you will find many more secrets that you are willing to reveal to the rest of us. As you do, may you never lose sight that your strength in teaching and mentoring is your ability to do and then teach.

May God help you to be good doers, so that your own one-man-one-woman relationship thrives and prospers for the good of your children and all who will be touched by this book.

Dr John Stanko
Author, Administrator,
President of PurposeQuest International
www.purposequest.com

PREFACE

Few things can enrich your life like a great relationship.

You can experience success in many areas of life, but without at least one meaningful relationship, you're left feeling hollow and empty. Yet, so many people are in dry, unfulfilling relationships lacking in intimacy. Despite their best efforts, they can't seem to make it work consistently. They find themselves making one step forward, two steps backward. They're left wondering, what are the secrets that a few couples tap into, while so many are left searching in the dark? ... Does this sound familiar?

I've found that for virtually anything that you desire in life, it's not the *external* changes that you make that will bring your desire to you. There are *internal* changes that you need to make first, and what you desire will be correspondingly drawn—or *attracted*—into your life.

Therefore, if you are in a relationship and you want more out of it, what are the internal changes that you need to make in order to pull or *attract* 'that relationship you dream of' into your existence?

Furthermore, if you're not in an intimate relationship and you'd like to be in one, what are the internal changes that you need to make in order to attract exactly what you want?

These are *the secrets of attraction* that I'll share with you in this book.

ৰুৰুৰুৰুৰুৰুৰুৰু

Think about it.

What is it that attracts a butterfly to a flower? It's the beautiful colour. The fragrance of its perfume. The anticipation of sweet nectar within. Just the same, decide to be the beautiful, fragrant flower that you are, and no matter where he[1] is hiding, soon 'your butterfly' will emerge, attracted to the essence of your being.

Incidentally, what an interesting metaphor of intimacy we find in nature. For

---

[1] I've written this book targeting females seeking greater intimacy in their relationship; if you're a man reading this book, just adjust the gender when necessary. This book will be just as beneficial to you.

just the same as the butterfly thrusts his proboscis deep into the belly of the flower to savour the sweet nectar within, so too, your partner and you can savour the 'sweet nectar' of your relationship based on complete intimacy: oneness in your body, mind, and spirit.

So, are you going to choose to be that flower?

Decide to be the beautiful, fragrant flower that you are, and no matter where he is hiding, soon 'your butterfly' will emerge, attracted to the essence of your being.

Remember, *you are in control.*

It's *your choice.*

Will you join the dance of nature and embrace the pleasure of oneness with your butterfly?

Or, will you join the masses who get a twisted satisfaction out of being dissatisfied? So many seem to derive perverted pleasure from complaining about the lack of good 'butterflies'....

Whatever you do, acknowledge from now that that the power of choice lies within you. You don't have to watch as a helpless bystander from the wayside of your life.

You can be in control *if* you discover *the secrets of attraction* and apply them to your relationship and life.

ぉぉぉぉぉぉぉぉ

So how do we successfully transform ourselves into that 'flower' and attract the desired butterfly?

One simple solution is to walk in the footprints of others' success!

Whatever you want in any area of your life—even intimacy in your significant relationship—find someone who's already experiencing it and model the principles of their success. *Adapt* and *adopt* what they've done to suit your specific situation.

There's one woman in the scriptures whose life breathes intimacy, particularly in her relationship with Jesus. I don't believe Jesus was sexually intimate with her or anyone else. But the secrets of attraction that she lived by were so powerful that even

Jesus opened up himself to her in a way that he did for no other woman.

And this really is what intimacy is all about—opening up yourself so that you can be one with another. Not just on a physical level, but baring your body, soul, and spirit to another. Allowing yourself to be naked, exposed, and vulnerable, with the mutual understanding that you're safe and unconditionally accepted.

This woman had such an effect on Jesus that he went to see her often. And he spent unhurried time with her, allowing her to handle him in a way that no other woman could. And should anyone criticize her, he quickly rose to her defence.

Who was this woman?

What was it about her that had this profound effect on Jesus?

What secrets can we learn from her, to arouse a similar response in the man of our life? Especially in this generation, in which painful, dysfunctional and broken relationships are the norm.

How can we use her example to heal our relationships?

ᘓᘓᘓᘓᘓᘓᘓᘓᘓ

The scriptures record at least three encounters between this woman and Jesus.

She is the quiet and unassuming Mary of Bethany, sister of Martha and Lazarus.

She has been a mentor for me in the 15-plus years of my marriage. And in a particularly challenging season of my marriage, I applied her secrets to tap into previously undiscovered levels of intimacy and fulfilment.

I *guarantee* that you will radically transform your relationship if you adopt any *one* of her powerful lifestyle habits. But, should you discover them all and inhale the fragrance of her life, you too will attract into your relationship all the intimacy and fulfilment that you've dreamed of.

Here's to your relationship success!

Heather Reid
Birmingham UK
September 2007
www.repositionyourlife.com

PS
If you're not yet in an intimate relationship, then don't wait until you're already in one to start preparing for it. *(Duh! ☺)* 'Arm' yourself from now with the secrets for your relationship success.

WHAT THEY'RE SAYING ABOUT THE SECRETS OF ATTRACTION

Heather walks the talk. If you apply the principles of this book, you will transform your relationship.
Dr Robert A Reid
Ophthalmic Surgeon
www.repositionyourlife.com

Well written. It is a long-awaited book that will prove to be very helpful…. Where's the next one?
Bishop Melvin A Brooks
Author, CEO of New Jerusalem Int'l Ministries
www.newj.org

Once I started reading, I could not put it down! I like the style of writing, enjoyed the humour, and appreciated the honesty. It is fresh, it is engaging, and easy to relate to.
Pastor Yvonne E Brooks
Author, Director - Women of Purpose Ministries
www.purposeministries.co.uk

Fantastic concept and angle from my perspective. Very well written and easy to understand. You done good!
Dr John Stanko
Author, Administrator, President of
PurposeQuest International
www.purposequest.com

A quick, very easy-going, entertaining read. The style is conversational and reads like a fireside chat with friends. It is informative and instructive, giving clear direction to the reader. I thoroughly enjoyed it.

Kevin Hutchinson
Computer Systems Analyst

Having read this book, I now have a new perspective of my husband. I've adjusted my working hours so that we can spend more time alone together. Thank you, Heather. This book was written for me.

Marie Anderson
Senior Legal Assistant

Wow! Wow! And wow again! It is amazing ... and that's just after reading the preface. Based on past hurts, I have feared getting close to anyone, just in case I'm hurt again. Just by reading the introduction to your book, I know this is an answer to my prayers.

Rose Anderson
Teacher, Psalmist, Music Consultant

My, my! What a wonderful experience. Typically, I find It difficult to finish a book, but I couldn't stop reading this until I came to the end. Wahoo! You talk about the 'taboo subject' so openly, relating it to scripture and the reality of our everyday lives. I am already making adjustments to my relationship. Thank you.

Thames Sylva
Counselor

CHAPTER ONE

MAKE THE MOST OF WHOM YOU'VE GOT

Have you ever compiled a mental list of all your partner's faults?

Have you ever thought how difficult it is to be in a relationship with him because of all his nasty habits? You wonder if it will ever be possible to experience the relationship you long for with your current partner....

Well consider this, *the quickest way to get what you want, is to be thankful for what you've already got!*

Instead of moaning about the faults of the one you're with, choose instead to make the most of him. Find something in him to be thankful about. There's really no such thing as 'the perfect man', and even if there were, you'd still have challenges in your relationship.

There are many who consider Jesus to be 'perfect'. Imagine for a minute that you were in a relationship with him... *Do you think it would be any easier?*

Pause for a moment.

What annoying habits might he have had?

First of all, Jesus was so intent on helping other people that he'd spend days on the road ministering to the masses. You could easily feel justified in thinking that he was neglecting you. Can you hear yourself complaining? "There he goes again: saving the world and neglecting me."

Otherwise, you could be niggled by his seeming insensitivity to people's needs. "What on earth were you thinking?" you could justifiably ask. "How could you talk to the people *soooooo* long: all day until late into the evening? Didn't you consider that they'd be hungry? Didn't you notice that there were women and children? What would you have done if that little boy hadn't taken a packed lunch? I'd have thought that a mature adult would be more responsible than that.... Didn't you plan ahead? *Ugggh!* Sometimes you make me so mad...."

On the other hand, you could see him as annoyingly laidback. Jesus was rarely ruffled. Nothing took him by surprise. Others would try to malign his character and he'd do nothing about it, sometimes, just squatting ignorantly, writing in the sand. It would be easy for you to nag, "God! You drive me crazy … you act as if you have no sense! Get some backbone, Jesus. Why don't you stand up for yourself? I thought you were a man—not a mouse!"

You could easily have fumed, "How could you have so much power, yet your friends have run out of wine at their wedding and you're doing nothing about it?"

Incidentally, even your mother-in-law (Jesus's mother, Mary) egged him on a bit, trying to get him to do something about the wine, only to have him retort, "Woman, what have I to do with you?"

What annoying habits might Jesus have had?

Furthermore, he'd frequently go off on his own, early in the morning to pray. You could easily demand that he have a lie-in with you more often.

Added to all of that, on numerous occasions Jesus would be deliberately tardy and use it as a means of glorifying God. But, from an irate and frustrated woman's perspective, he could easily be seen as un-ambitious, undependable, and inconsiderate.

And, to top it all, because Jesus was omniscient, you could finally explode one day that he was such a *whatsitnotsit* know-it-all.

৵৵৵৵৵৵৵৵৵৵

Fact is, no matter whom you're with, it's *inevitable* that you'll have challenges in your relationship. It's how you choose to handle those challenges that matter.

The grass may look greener over the fence, but it still needs to be mowed! So, it makes no sense to hop from relationship to relationship hoping that you'll find the 'right man'. Neither is it any better to be stuck in a dead relationship, harbouring hurt feelings, un-forgiveness, and bitterness.

> **It's perfectly normal to have challenges in your relationship no matter whom you're with. So when they arise don't start looking for greener fields—learn to take care of your own garden first.**

Instead, make the most of whom you've got. Acknowledge that he is the unique creation of Almighty God who loves him with an unconditional love. *Yes*, even with all his faults! So, if God can so love your partner, there just might be something in him that makes it worthwhile for you to love him too!

Furthermore, God interprets how you respond to your partner as a clear indication of how you respond to him. Whatever you do to your partner (or, really, any other person) is what you're doing to God himself.[2] The attitudes that you display toward your partner, are the attitudes you're showing toward God.

So, in a manner of speaking, your relationship *is* with 'Jesus'! Your partner, like Jesus, is a manifestation of God! He may not be as perfectly aligned with God as Jesus, but you still need to respond to your partner with the love and respect that you show to the Lord.

And, most importantly, *believe* that it is possible for you to have a relationship based on lasting intimacy, trust, and mutual desire. Make a *decision* that separation or divorce does not exist for you. And that you'll accept and expect nothing less than mutual fulfilment in your relationship.

---

[2] **Matthew 25:40** *Inasmuch as ye have done it unto one of the least of these my brethren, ye have done it unto me.*

Now for a bit of 'chit chat' to make this *secret of attraction* real. I'll use real examples from my own experience, to help you apply these secrets in your own life.

When I first met my husband-to-be 22 years ago at university, it was 'love at first sight!' But *definitely not* in the way that you may be thinking. I met him and immediately concluded that he was the *'ugliest male creature'* I had ever set eyes on. And on top of that, he had 'country bumpkin' oozing out his every pore.

His trousers were 'retro' long before retro ever became fashionable. And I could describe his t-shirt only as *'heng-pan-mi'*.[3] "Ugh," I thought, "I'll never be caught dead with him!"

But in that same moment, an inner prompting overtook those thoughts and challenged me instead to love him as Christ would. Reluctantly I 'humbled myself', yielded to the Spirit's inner direction, and started a conversation with Robert....

In my opinion at the time, there was no trace of handsome-ness in his face. If I mimic a

---

[3] Transliteration for the Jamaican expression 'heng pan mi' is 'hangs on me'—in other words, stretched out and misshaped.

quote from the scriptures, there was *no beauty in him that I should desire him...!* There was just *no indication*—in the Robert whom I first met—of the strength and beauty of his character. Nor of the gentleman, leader and superb husband and father that he was to become.

So, I've never regretted that day when I submitted to the Spirit's lead. I applied this secret of attraction, making the most of whom Robert was then. I chose to perceive the potential in my partner-to-be. Over time, I've helped to nurture (or *attract*) into existence the man who he is today. *(Or maybe I flatter myself to believe that!)*

At any rate, I'll continue to make the most of whom I've got—warts and all!

How about you?

SUMMARY

- There is no 'perfect man'.

- No matter whom you're with—even if it was Jesus—there will be challenges in your relationship. Challenges are a perfectly normal part of every relationship.

- It's how you respond to those challenges that really matter. Choose to cultivate an attitude of thankfulness. The quickest way to get what you want is to be thankful for what (and whom) you've already got.

- Choose to perceive the potential in your partner and attract him into existence by constantly making the most of whom you've got.

APPLICATION

- If you could design the 'perfect relationship', what would it be like?

- What would your partner be like?

- What kind of lifestyle would you enjoy together?

- What new hobbies would you try together?

- OK. Get back to reality. You know who you're with. What 'baby-steps' can you take today to move yourself in the direction of your perfect relationship?

CHAPTER TWO

ONE THING'S NEEDED

In his dealings with Mary, Jesus reveals that there is *one critical ingredient* for the success of your relationship. Without it, all else pales into insignificance. What could it be? Read on to discover.

On one particular occasion, Mary was in her sister Martha's house.[4] They were

---

[4] The encounter is outlined in **Luke 10:38-42**, which reads: *Now it came to pass, as they went, that he entered into a certain village: and a certain woman named Martha received him into her house. And she had a sister called Mary, which also sat at Jesus' feet, and heard his word. But Martha was cumbered about much serving, and came to him, and said, Lord, dost thou not care that my*

expecting a visit from Jesus. Martha was busy in the kitchen sorting out the meal, when Jesus stepped through the door.

Instead of simply stopping to welcome and enjoy him, Martha threw herself into the work more intensely, wanting to serve the meal with excellence.

By the time she got to the lounge and saw Mary: cool, composed, and cozy with *her* guest, she just lost it!

"How on earth can you allow my sister just to sit there doing nothing?" she demanded, having stormed in, arms akimbo, sweaty and disheveled. "And you let her leave me to slave in the kitchen on my own? Send her to come and help me!"

Can you hear the venom in her voice?

Jesus could easily have felt she was challenging his authority and authenticity. She might as well have said, "If you were the Christ that you claim to be, surely you would've sent my sister in to help me!"

How many times do you have this acidic attitude toward your partner, just because—for the moment—you do not understand or agree with his actions?

---

sister hath left me to serve alone? bid her therefore that she help me. And Jesus answered and said unto her, Martha, Martha, thou art careful and troubled about many things: But one thing is needful: and Mary hath chosen that good part, which shall not be taken away from her.

Jesus calmly replied, "Martha ... Martha ... " Finally, she calmed down enough to listen to him.

"You're far too concerned with the minor details that really don't matter. *Only one thing is needed* and Mary has made that good choice."

What could that 'one thing' be?

Do you remember the principle? Seek him first then all the other things will be sorted.

I believe the 'one thing' that Jesus referred to is the absolute importance of seeking him first. [5] Not just in external acts of service, but *spending unhurried time alone with him.*

When you spend time alone with him consistently, it helps you to hear and recognize his voice. And you've already seen from the 'chit-chat' at the end of the previous chapter, what dividends it pays when you recognize and obey his voice, and not just follow your own understanding.

Regardless of all your short-term and long-term goals, regardless of what's on the day's to-do list, focusing on Jesus and what pleases him is the 'one thing' that you *must*

---

[5] That's based on the principle laid out in **Matthew 6:33**—*Seek ye first the kingdom of God, and his righteousness; and all these things shall be added unto you.*

do. And, like Mary, whether or not you do it, is your choice.

Jesus is the ultimate source of success in your relationship. So that's the single most important thing that you can do to preserve and prosper it.

But there's more to it than that!

This whole thing of love between a man and a woman—really, a man and his wife—is a metaphor of the love between the Lord Jesus and his church (i.e., those who've surrendered their heart and committed their life to him).[6]

So how you relate to your partner—in particular, your husband—should mirror how you relate to your Lord.

Regardless of how long your to-do list is, and what you haven't yet done, make sure that you do this one thing everyday: *spend time alone with your partner focusing on what pleases him.* It takes time to build intimate and fulfilling relationships.

Even if you're physically apart, do it over the phone!

---

[6] Jesus is committed to his church *unconditionally* for life, and he'll let nothing and no one get in the way. Just in the same way that he reserves the outpouring of his spirit for those who've made a lifelong commitment to him, so too should a man reserve the 'outpouring of his substance' until he's made a commitment to one woman for life, through marriage.

Here's a bit of 'chit chat' especially relevant if you're still single.

Over 20 years ago my husband-to-be Robert first proposed, with a beautiful parchment card, that we start a relationship. We were very close friends but I was definitely not attracted to him in that way. I couldn't honestly accept his proposal for such a relationship. And I didn't.

Yet, when I had prayed about it, the Holy Spirit didn't allow me to say no to Robert's proposal. But as much as I wanted to obey the Spirit's prompting, I refused to say yes to someone I didn't desire. I was actually *'shocked out of my wits'* during that prayer, because—as friendly as we were—Robert was one of the *last* persons that I'd dream of marrying, and I had no desire to be in a relationship with him.

I didn't disclose my encounter in prayer to Robert, but merely told him, "Thanks, but I don't see you in that way." In retrospect, he must have been heartbroken. But he didn't selfishly withdraw himself from me, or go looking for someone else. Based on our friendship, he continued to spend quite a lot of time with me. His choice paid dividends.

Things began to work in Robert's favour, because that summer my protective suburban mother, asked Robert to be a 'chaperone' for me.

www.repositionyourlife.com

She wasn't happy with all the church-related activities I was doing in volatile inner-city communities, and felt much better knowing that I was accompanied by a strong young man with Christian values.

I had never spent so much time with any one person. We talked as we rode on the buses and walked along the streets. At times when the buses were overcrowded (which was quite a frequent occurrence) I couldn't help but notice how comfortable I felt with the closeness of our bodies.

We prayed together, read the scriptures together, laughed with each other, and ate lunch together. We experienced fear together—as a pedestrian fired shots onto a bus that we were traveling in, and the conductor wielded his machete in self-defence ... Robert literally 'carried me to safety'—my own knight in shining armour! And we experienced the exhilaration of a not-too-narrow escape. *I've never told this to my parents; let's hope they're not reading!* ☺

I had always wished I was from a large family, then I met all Robert's eight siblings and visited his parents who lived on a farm in cool hills of the beautiful countryside—a welcome retreat from the tropical suburban heat. That did it. I was smitten. *(And I still am!)*

What a difference one summer made! Just spending *unhurried time alone* with Robert completely altered my perception of him. I had a chance to observe how he naturally operated in different settings, unlike before when I saw him only at university or church. I certainly liked what I saw!

So, be willing to spend time with the 'right character'. Someone who will respect your values and boundaries, and not try to take advantage of you. Even if at first he doesn't see your virtues—or you don't see his. Don't completely rule him out. Give him time. It could work wonders for you both.

GOOD OL' HOME COOKIN'

In order to please and empower the typical man, you need to make time to sincerely *acknowledge, appreciate,* and *adore* him.

Slow down!

Make it happen.

Don't be derailed by the busy-ness and dizziness of modern-day lifestyles.

Everyday he must be made to feel and know that he's your 'lord and king', your friend, your lover ... your everything!

Don't be one of the masses of women who're ignorant of this secret, overly concerned with the mundane, daily demands of life. Do the 'one thing' that's needed. Seek him first. Prioritize time alone with him focusing on his needs. Soon enough, you'll find that a whole lot of other things in your relationship will be sorted, including putting out the rubbish and a load of odd jobs on your to-do list.

Incidentally, while most men appreciate a good *home-cooked meal*, even more do they value a good '*home-cooked woman*'! So, keep your partner 'well-fed' at home and he'll be too full to consider 'eating out'.

Like Jesus did with Mary, he'll commend and defend you, even when other women, like Martha, try to highlight your flaws.

WHAT'S NO. 1 FOR THE TYPICAL MAN?

Like it or not, what's on the mind of the typical man in an intimate relationship is sex. Frequent, enthusiastic, and interesting sex is always 'top of the pops'.

If your partner is a typical male and he says otherwise, be careful: he'll lie about other things too!

There is a fundamental difference in how men and women view sex. Not understanding this has caused endless pain in many relationships, including mine—until I discovered *the secrets of attraction.*

Let's cover some basics first: sexual intercourse allows the typical man to release the sexual tension that builds up naturally in him every day as a result of his own hormonal changes. It's simply a natural, physical need. Just like you need to breathe. *You're not obsessed with oxygen ... neither is he obsessed with sex.*

When the typical man is unable to have sex as often as he desires in his relationship, he is similar to many pre-menstrual women: edgy, irritable, snappy, and stressed!

On the other hand, the typical woman doesn't have *daily* cycles but rather *monthly* cycles in her hormonal changes. These lead to peaks and troughs in the typical woman's sexual desire over the course of a month. This is radically different from the typical man's constant 'testosteronic'-high.

For any mature man in a committed, long term, monogamous relationship, sex isn't just a superficial 'wham-bam'—even if it seems that way to you. Rather, it is a deep, meaningful expression allowing for the physical, emotional and spiritual bonding of a man with his woman.

COMMUNICATION vs SEX?

The typical woman will argue that what's most important in an intimate relationship is communication[7] and companionship. But we've already seen how important sex is to the typical man.

This difference of what's considered number one in an intimate relationship causes numerous conflicts.

Too few women understand this basic difference in how men and women perceive communication and sex.

Learn this secret, and you'll uncover one major cause of separation and divorce.

Generally, *a woman needs ongoing expressions of love, tenderness, and romance to heighten her desire for sex.* Most women assume that this is how it is for all humans. But there's approximately half of the human population that perceives things differently!

For the typical man, the complete opposite is true.

A man needs sex to heighten his desire to express love, tenderness, and romance.

While the importance of communication in any relationship is undebatable, sex is an indisputable lubricant that 'oils the hinges' of the typical man. Keep your man 'well-greased', and you'll see how much easier it is for him to 'open up'.

---

[7] It's said that the four words that men dread hearing the most from their partners are, "We need to talk."

Until a couple is willing to acknowledge this difference in how they're 'wired' and adjust their lifestyles accordingly, then sexual incompatibility and lack of fulfilment will be the over-riding flavour of the day.

Women need ongoing expressions of love, tenderness, and romance to heighten their desire for sex.

Men need ongoing sex to heighten their desire to express love, tenderness, and romance.

Unfortunately, the situation is worse for many Christian women who harbour the misconception that Christian men are—or ought to be—different. Get a dose of reality. *No matter how Spirit-filled, anointed, or Christ-like they are, men love sex.* So, don't make the mistake of withholding sex from your partner.

Think of your partner like a typical modern car. With the right fuel and *regular servicing*, it will serve you well. Otherwise, it may leave you stranded on the road.

Here's a bit more 'chit chat' with a very personal experience. I've never believed in hiding behind the cloak of 'super-spirituality'—I believe in 'being real'. So, I'll reveal some 'secrets' from my own life....

How clearly I remember 15 years ago when I lost my status of '*chaste* virgin' and acquired the new status of '*chased* wife'. It seemed to me then that I was constantly 'pursued' by my husband, Robert, for *one thing*.

We got married in the Caribbean at 7:30 in the morning. I naively assumed we were getting married that early so we could savour the cool freshness of a tropical morning. Robert evidently had other motives up his sleeve—*or trousers!*

While I naively anticipated the joy of sharing my *life* with Robert, it became clear to me, after one week of honeymoon, that Robert had been anticipating the joy of sharing his *bed*—or just about any other surface that was handy....

After recovering from my honeymoon, I seriously wondered, was my husband trying to impress me with his masculinity? I concede—I was duly impressed. The novelty of it all was enthralling! It was fascinating to explore each other physically and otherwise. And Robert seemed to live by the motto 'make hay while the sun shines'. And so, living in the tropics as we did, we made a lot of hay! *Ha!*

Eventually, I figured it was time for us to 'calm down' and settle back into a 'normal lifestyle'.

Only then did the realization hit me, that what I thought was 'abnormal sexual frenzy' was not just the temporary side effect of a fantastic honeymoon. Neither was it just a short-lived phase of a previously sex-starved virgin male. It finally dawned on me that for Robert—like any typical man—that was a 'normal lifestyle'.

Unfortunately for me, based on my sheltered upbringing, it took me years of tears and prayers to overcome my mental programming—all the subconscious beliefs and expectations that I had held from my childhood.

I finally learned to *accept* that Robert was 'normal'. I had to *acknowledge* that it was God who made him that way and that I didn't need to try to 'get' him to change. (I'd have failed anyway.) Rather, I needed to *adjust* my lifestyle to ensure that my husband (like my 'modern car') got the right kind of fuel and *regular servicing!* I had no intentions of being left stranded on the road.

7 REASONS WHY YOU SHOULD NOT REJECT YOUR PARTNER'S SEXUAL ADVANCES

1. The scriptures say you shouldn't! **1 Corinthians 7:4-5** *The wife hath not power of her own body, but the husband: and likewise also the husband hath not power of his own body, but the wife. Defraud* [or deprive] *ye not the other....* It never pays to go against any scriptural recommendation for your relationship.

2. When you reject *sex*, your partner interprets that you're rejecting *him*.

3. After a good 'round of sex', your partner faces the world—despite all its pressures and stresses—feeling like the master of the universe.

4. Action creates motivation. One big hurdle to achievement is *starting*. Ignore the initial inertia of 'not feeling in the mood' and just start the process. Once the 'momentum' kicks in, it's likely you'll thoroughly enjoy it!

5. If you're rejecting your partner's sexual advances because you're sincerely tired, it's often far more wearisome to deal

with his disappointment; it's much simpler to offer him a 'quickie'. The same goes if you're rejecting his sexual advances because of a genuine headache—it's often more of a headache to deal with the aftermath of sexual rejection, than to offer a quickie.

6. If you're really not enjoying sex with him ... if his breath or underarm smells, if he ejaculates prematurely leaving you high and dry or wet and upset, if his foreplay skills are lacking, or if he doesn't know where or what a clitoris is ... then rejecting his sexual advances is *not* solving the problem. Initiate loving, respectful, and open conversation. Honesty is the root of intimacy. Say it right and the typical man will be *turned on* that you're open about your sexual preferences and that you want to enjoy sex with him.

7. If you repeatedly reject your partner's advances, he'll soon lose interest in you, and there'll be at least seven other women who'll gladly accept him in your stead.

SUMMARY

- The 'one thing' you need to do is seek God first, prioritizing time alone with him; he's the source of success in your relationship.

- Your relationship with your partner should mimic your relationship with your Lord. Prioritize unhurried time alone with him everyday focusing on his needs—including his need for sex.

- When you do this, your partner will be far more focused on pleasing you.

APPLICATION

- Although Jesus was called Lord, in many ways, he was like any other man. He had a 'combination lock' and if you discovered his code, you could trigger him to open up his heart to you and reveal the pathway to intimacy, communion, and oneness with him.

- What is it that makes your partner 'tick'? Do you know the code for his combination lock?

- Are you using it?

CHAPTER THREE

TAKE ANOTHER LOOK

What if you have absolutely no desire to prioritize time alone with your partner? It may be that you've lost the desire to focus on his needs because you're frustrated, unfulfilled, and feeling your relationship is past its best-by date.

Don't worry, you're not alone. You're not the first to feel that way and you certainly won't be the last.

There's no need to end your relationship. I believe that's taking the easy way out. That's the way of weaklings! I prefer instead to have some guts. 'Fight' for what you want. Stick it out. See it through. But, you don't want to stick it out in a stale, stagnant relationship either. No way! It's not worth it. Not for the sake of children, church, or whoever.

Pause.

Breathe.

Step back.

Take another look.

A 90-year-old couple walked into their solicitor's office and announced that they wanted to file for a divorce after 70 years of marriage. "But you lasted this long," said their surprised solicitor. "Why divorce now?" The couple flatly responded, "We were waiting for the kids to die."

Quite often you feel *'out-of-love'* because you're *'out-of-focus'*.

Check yourself.

Are you missing the diamond in your partner, because of the dirt you have to dig through?

Are you living like Martha? Feeling frustrated 'cause you're focused on the fact that Jesus didn't send Mary to help you.

Or do you observe Mary's *secret of attraction?* Finding fulfilment by focusing on the love that moved Jesus to spend unhurried time with you.

You create your reality by your focus.

And whatever you focus on grows.

What's your focus?

Frustration or fulfilment?

Dirt or diamonds?

What's your focus for your partner?
The dirt? Or the diamond?

If you zoom in on the faults of the man you're with, that's what will dominate your relationship.

> **Are you missing the diamond in your partner, because of the dirt you need to dig through?**

It's so easy to get caught up with his flaws, even minor ones—socks in his shoes, crumbs in the kitchen, fuzz in the face basin—that all his positive traits fade into insignificance....

> **See a man as he is and he'll remain as he is.**
>
> **See a man as he can become and he'll grow to fill your expectations of him.**
>
> **My adaptation of Goethe's quote.**

How about focusing on his positive traits for a change?

How about focusing on his potential?

How about focusing on the diamond?

When you do, you will respond to him more positively, and he will then respond to the-more-positive-you more positively. You will then respond even more positively to the more-positive-him! And ... need I go on? Ultimately, you'll create an upward spiral of 'positivity' in your relationship.

Have you ever heard the true story Acres of Diamond?

A man died a wretched pauper having sold his farm to go in search of elusive diamonds.

The purchaser of his plot of land later found a magnificent diamond-mine, right there on the farm. From this same plot of land were mined many of the existing crown jewels.

What diamonds lay undiscovered in your 'farm'—or snoring in your bedroom?

Some years ago when I was a stay-at-home mother of two, Robert's career would require him to be out of the house for long, irregular hours—sometimes it was before our sons woke up and after they'd gone to bed.

So Robert chose to make breakfast for our sons each morning. When they woke up, even if he'd already left for work, they'd know that their Daddy had made breakfast for them.

And he'd make elaborate breakfasts: hot dogs, creamy cornmeal porridge, toasted pita bread, tortilla wraps, or omelettes with various savoury fillings....

After Robert left for work, I was the one who'd serve the breakfast to our sons. And I'd be *fuming*....

Because I didn't have the clear perspective then that I do *now*, of just how helpful Robert was trying to be. Rather, I had a very limited perspective because of my tunnel-vision focus. All I could see were the crumbs on the cutting board, or the cheese that wasn't put back in the fridge, or the utensils left on the shelf....

On and on I'd mentally murmur, complaining to myself while I cleaned up. There I was, bottling it all up until it blew out of proportion. I was incensed because of Robert's *extreme insensitivity and untidiness*—or that's what I perceived it to be. And my perception—like yours—was my reality.

Until finally one day, I calmed down, stepped back, reconsidered, and got a broader perspective. My husband—an Ophthalmic Surgeon—would often get home from work in the wee hours of the morning, having had very little sleep after a very busy 24- or 48-hour on-call. Then he'd have another full day of work starting early the next morning. (That was then the reality of his job in the British National Health Service!)

Anyway, in that window of time at home, Robert could've easily opted to get dressed and get out. But he chose instead to spend time with me, put out the rubbish, do other odd jobs, plus make our sons' breakfast, before taking the half-hour commute to work. How could I have been so insensitive?

When I changed my focus, everything changed. I became more *appreciative* and therefore more *appealing* in his eyes. He was therefore even more willing to please the more-appealing-me. It was literally a 'vital cycle' of positivity.

Sure, it would've been nicer if Robert consistently cleaned up. And I'm not saying that leaving crumbs behind is okay. But what was not okay was focusing on 'crumbs in the kitchen' with self-centred ungratefulness while completely missing my husband's consistently selfless kindness.

It may not be something as simple as crumbs in the kitchen for you, but whatever it is, take another look. Choose your focus.

SUMMARY

- Change your relationship by changing your focus.

- You create your reality by your focus.

APPLICATION

Take a fresh look at your partner. Write your answers to the following questions.

- Reminisce on the early days when you 'fell' in love and felt in love; what were the traits that first attracted you to him?

- How has he grown since then?

- What are some of the current positive traits about your partner, including the ordinary, common, everyday characteristics that you easily take for granted?

- What are some of the horrible traits that he could have, but doesn't?

- How do other people—whose opinion you value—see your partner? Sometimes you're so intensely immersed and emotionally entangled in your relationship that you're not seeing clearly.

- How do other women—whose opinion you don't value—see your partner? Don't let the diamond slip through your fingers. If you do, there are seven other women who will quickly jump for it!

CHAPTER FOUR

MIND YOUR MOUTH

Let's look at another revealing encounter between Jesus and Mary.[8]

---

[8] It's found in **John 11:1-44.** Here are some excerpts:

Now a certain man was sick, named Lazarus, of Bethany, the town of Mary and her sister Martha. Therefore his sisters sent unto him, saying, Lord, behold, he whom thou lovest is sick.

Now Jesus loved Martha, and her sister, and Lazarus. When he had heard therefore that he was sick, he abode two days still in the same place where he was.

...Then after that saith he to his disciples, Let us go into Judaea again. His disciples say unto him, Master, the Jews of late sought to stone thee; and goest thou thither again?

...When Jesus came, he found that he had lain in the grave four days already.

Then Martha, as soon as she heard that Jesus was coming, went and met him: but Mary sat still in the house.

Then said Martha unto Jesus, Lord, if thou hadst been here, my brother had not died. But I know, that even now, whatsoever thou wilt ask of God, God will give it thee. Jesus saith unto her, Thy brother shall rise again. Martha saith unto him, I know that he shall rise again in the resurrection at the last day. Jesus said unto her, I am the resurrection, and the life: he that believeth in me, though he were dead, yet shall he live: And whosoever liveth and believeth in me shall never die. Believest thou this? She saith unto him, Yea, Lord: I believe that thou art the Christ, the Son of God, which should come into the world.

And when she had so said, she went her way, and called Mary her sister secretly, saying, The Master is come, and calleth for thee.

As soon as she heard that, she arose quickly, and came unto him.

Now Jesus was not yet come into the town, but was in that place where Martha met him ... when Mary was come where Jesus was, and saw him, she fell down at his feet, saying unto him, Lord, if thou hadst been here, my brother had not died.

When Jesus therefore saw her weeping, and the Jews also weeping which came with her, he groaned in the spirit, and was troubled, And said, Where have ye laid him?

They said unto him, Lord, come and see.

Jesus wept.

Jesus therefore ... cometh to the grave. It was a cave, and a stone lay upon it. Jesus said, Take ye away the stone.

Martha, the sister of him that was dead, saith unto him, Lord, by this time he stinketh: for he hath been dead four days.

Jesus saith unto her, Said I not unto thee, that, if thou wouldest believe, thou shouldest see the glory of God?

Then they took away the stone from the place where the dead was laid. And Jesus ... cried with a loud

Mary and Martha's brother Lazarus had developed a serious health problem, so they'd sent for Jesus.

Based on the closeness of their friendship, they expected that he'd come right away to heal his friend.

However, Jesus delayed.

He waited a couple days before heading out. When he finally got to Bethany where they lived, Lazarus was already dead, buried, and rotting.

To cut a long story short, Jesus deliberately delayed, using the opportunity to glorify God. Instead of merely healing Lazarus, Jesus raised him from the dead!

Sounds great to us in *hindsight*, but at the time, Mary and Martha didn't know his plan. To them he could've seemed plain inconsiderate. Cruel. Heartless.

Let's see how they handled this situation.

෨෨෨෨෨෨෨෨෨

As soon as Martha heard Jesus was coming, she rushed out to meet him.

As in the previous encounter, there was no warm greeting, no loving embrace,

---

voice, Lazarus, come forth. And he that was dead came forth.

and no expression of thanks that he bothered to come at all. Especially since coming to Bethany would've put his life at risk, as it was so near to Jerusalem where the Jews wanted to kill him.

Instead, there was a barrage of accusations. "If you were here, my brother would not have died!"

She hurled another verbal missile, "Even now, if only you would ask, God would do it for you."

Jesus responded, "Your brother shall rise again."

Annoyed at Jesus's calmness, Martha snapped, "I know he'll rise again in the resurrection at the last day." She was probably thinking, "Sure he'll rise on the *last day*, but I want him alive *now!*"

Jesus reminded her that he was the resurrection and the life, and that anyone who died believing in him would live. He asked her if she believed this.

"Yes," she answered. But, apparently, things weren't going quite the way that she wanted, so, without another word, she rushed off to fetch Mary.

In the last encounter, Martha tried to 'get' Jesus to 'get' Mary to help her. Now she's about to try to 'get' Mary to 'get' Jesus to do something about Lazarus. Sounds like a bit of a control freak.

Are you applying Martha's tactics? Are you manipulative? What are you trying to 'get' your partner to do?

Martha secretly called her sister, whispering, "Jesus has come and he's calling for you."

Jesus hadn't really arrived in Bethany yet, and there's no indication that he was calling for Mary.

As soon as Mary got Martha's message she too arose quickly from grieving in the house and went straight to Jesus.

On finding Jesus, Mary's words were identical to her sister's, "If you were here, my brother wouldn't have died."

But her attitude was completely different.

How can you know this?

Check what she did: while she spoke to Jesus, she fell at his feet. In her day, this posture showed an attitude of gratitude,

> **How do you approach your partner when you feel completely disappointed in his actions?**
> **With hot-headed anger and accusations? Guilty until proven innocent? Or with trust that he's somehow innocent until he confesses to be guilty?**

adoration, and worship.

It's not only 'what' you say that matters, but 'how' you say it.

And so Jesus's response to Mary was very different from his previous response to Martha.

With Martha, he responded with words. You could say, *Jesus argued back.* Not with impatience or anger, because he loved Martha, but he calmly argued back.

But with Mary, when Jesus felt her adoration as she fell at his feet and saw her (and the onlookers) weeping, he groaned in his spirit and was troubled. He had no desire to *argue*, but to *act.*

Immediately he found out where Lazarus was and gave instructions that the stone over Lazarus's tomb be taken away.

Once again, Martha's 'killer tongue' sprung to action, continuing to argue even while Jesus was attending to the problem.

"Lord!" she exclaimed, "Lazarus has been dead for four days; by this time he stinks!"

How many times do you continue to argue, even after your partner has begun to do the very thing that you wanted him to?

Once again, Martha's approach doesn't yield action from Jesus, only 'argument'. Jesus questioned Martha, "Didn't

I say to you that, if you would believe, you should see the glory of God?"

**Scientific research shows that we remember only 10-20% of what we hear, but far more of what we see and feel.
Therefore, you're wasting your breath when you talk non-stop:
he'll forget over half of what you say!**

But he won't forget how he *felt* when you said it.

Having dealt with Martha's interruption, Jesus finally proceeded to call Lazarus from the dead.

Jesus (like any typical man!) was turned off by non-stop nagging.

By the way, did you know that what you speak and how you speak is a matter of *life and death?*[9]

Your tongue can make or break your relationship for your words are self-fulfilling prophecies, particularly when spoken with strong conviction.

---

[9] **Proverbs 18:21** *Death and life are in the power of the tongue: and they that love it shall eat the fruit thereof.*

What you speak and how you speak are based on the thoughts and feelings that you harbour in your heart.[10] And the thoughts that you harbour determine who you are.[11]

So you need to carefully monitor and manage your thoughts and emotions. When you feel overtaken by negative feelings, *you still don't have a right to launch a verbal attack.* You still need to control your mouth and choose your words carefully.

What kind of thoughts are you harbouring about your partner?

Love, trust, and acceptance?

Or fear, doubt, and rejection?

What are you speaking?

Life? Or death?

Do your words thrill? Or kill?

෴෴෴෴෴

By the way, if you're not yet in a relationship, are you speaking 'death' by declaring: "There are no good men left—they're either already married, in prison, or gay...."? If you keep saying that often enough, you'll eat the fruit

---

[10] **Mark 12:34** and **Luke 6:45** both say: *out of the abundance of the heart the mouth speaketh.*

[11] **Proverbs 23:7**— *as he* [or she] *thinketh in his* [or her] *heart, so is he* [or she].

of your lips: they'll be no good men left for you.

There's a couple I knew some years ago—let's call them Chris and Samantha to preserve their privacy. Samantha really ate the fruit of her lips, and is still doing so now.

Before they both became Christians, she used to be paranoid, always fearful that her husband was seeing another woman. She would repeatedly question him about it, or accuse him of being unfaithful. Despite his assurances that no such thing was happening, the interrogation continued.

After a while, Chris was fed up, knowing that he was being true to his woman unlike many of his mates at the time. He was so annoyed with Samantha that the next time the opportunity presented 'herself', he did sleep with another woman. His value system at the time did not constrain him from doing so. Not only did he have an affair with her, but he also had a baby with the other woman.

Years later, when working it through with Samantha, Chris said the thing that really goaded him into sleeping with another woman was her constant questions and accusations about his unfaithfulness.

A TONGUE THAT KILLS:

Jumps straight to negative accusations (a bit like Martha did with Jesus).

Argues in front of the children, neighbours, and colleagues under-mining her partner's authority.

Shouts.

Bottles up issues, avoids confrontation and then without warning ... explodes!

Attacks and belittles her partner in an argument, using name-calling or expletives.

Takes courtesies for granted, refusing to 'waste' the effort of using words like 'please' and 'thank you' on her partner.

Seeks to have her way, all the time.

Nags.

Often uses sexual blackmail: "No sex for you until this matter is sorted." Even if she doesn't say it in so many words, her actions (or inactivity) say it loud and clear.

A TONGUE THAT THRILLS:

Starts and ends every discussion positively, using body language— not just words.

Affirms her partner in front of all onlookers, building confidence and camaraderie.

Does not shout.

Has regular, open discussions, not only when crises develop; gets to the point, emphasizing positive not negative issues.

Attacks the problem, not her partner. Focuses on the issue being discussed, and on finding a solution.

Consistently uses basic courtesies like 'please' and 'thank you' to make sure her partner knows he's valued.

Seeks a mutually acceptable solution, acknowledging that her partner is entitled to have different opinions, methods, etc.

Stops talking once the problem is solved ... or even before.

Doesn't let the sun go down on her wrath nor let an argument get between her and her partner, in or out of bed.

So, what do you do when you're feeling hot-headed anger toward your partner, and you feel you need to 'set him straight' right away?

I have an excellent eight-point model for handling conflict in your relationship. I deal with it in Chapter 6, Choose Your Company. But, before you can effectively apply that model and deal with heated differences in your relationship, you first need to discover another important secret.

Without mastering this secret, your hope for intimacy and mutual fulfillment in your relationship is doomed for failure. Read on to the next chapter to find out more.

SUMMARY

- Let your mind control your mouth.

- Cultivate a mindset based on attitudes of love, oneness, acceptance, and trust.

- Decide beforehand what attitudes you'll entertain towards your partner, regardless of how you perceive his actions. You can't afford to 'fly off the handle' saying just anything that comes to your head based on your ever-changing feelings.

APPLICATION

- Think about times in the past that your partner has acted contrary to your expectations. Maybe he didn't put out the week's rubbish, or he stayed out late unexpectedly and didn't call.

- What's your typical response?

- Do you assume he's guilty until proven innocent?

- Do you accost your partner based on the immediate feelings of hot-headed anger, suspicion, fear, or doubt?

- Keep a journal and monitor your ongoing thoughts, assumptions, and attitudes toward your partner, with a view to improving them.

CHAPTER FIVE

MIND YOUR EARS

Every human being, even your partner, yearns for self-expression. A chance to give vent. To be heard. To be understood. To have an audience. We all crave at least one person who cares enough to listen non-judgmentally to what we have to say. When you acknowledge this need and provide that non-judgmental listening ear, you'll *open wide* the door to intimacy in your relationship.

Mary was in tune with Jesus's need when he visited Martha's house and she listened attentively to his every word.

Believe it or not, your partner—like Jesus—longs to talk.

Are you missing this opportunity for intimacy by focusing on your own need to talk and trying to 'get' your partner to listen?

Or, are you trying too hard to 'get' your partner to talk?

You'll never successfully 'get' him to do anything.

Even if you do, he'll do so grudgingly—whether he's resentfully listening to your rambling or coughing up monosyllables in response to your interrogation. He's not doing it out of his own will or desire, but rather, he's just giving in to your pressure.

Surely there must be a better way.

There is!

It's simple.

Pause for a moment.

Think about how much you want to express yourself, sometimes to the extent that you'll interrupt someone else who's speaking, or your mind strays from what's being said to think instead about how you want to respond.

Next, think about how you feel when you do find someone who'll listen, whom you can trust.... You're ready to pour your heart out. You sometimes reveal far more than you ever intended to. And once you're through, you feel indebted to the listener. Invariably, you begin to wonder how you can repay....

It's no different for your partner.

When you're consistently willing to listen to him, he'll be far more willing to listen to you. He'll also be far more willing to bare his heart to you.

In just the same way that you need to 'mind your mouth' (see Chapter 4), so too you need to 'mind your ears'—be careful how you listen, exercising self-control and discipline.

Unfortunately, most of us are poor listeners. *It's much easier to focus on the conversation in our own head or to prepare our rebuttal, than to listen to what another person is saying.*

Listening is a conscious choice. Particularly the level of listening that leads to intimacy. It's a deliberate act that requires discipline and focus.

There are eight skills that you need to master in order to listen effectively—the kind of listening that builds intimacy in your relationship.

1. EYE CONTACT

Look directly into your partner's eyes as he speaks to you and be sensitive to his mood. Yet too much eye contact can be overpowering and unsettling. Use it in a natural way.

Think about when you're speaking to someone. If his eyes keep straying to see what's happening elsewhere in the room, it sends the message that he's not too interested in the conversation, and, perhaps, not too interested in you. You don't want to give that message to your partner.

If you're really not interested in your partner or his conversation, then re-read Chapter 3, Take Another Look.

2. POSTURE

Mary chose her posture well.

When Jesus came to dinner, she sat at his feet. No distractions could come between him and her.

At her brother's death, she approached Jesus bowing down in adoration. Jesus had no doubts as to how she felt about him. Though her words could imply that she was challenging his tardiness, he got her message through her posture of love and commitment.

Just the same, you'll want to make sure your posture makes a statement!

If you watch the body language of those attracted to each other, they naturally gravitate toward each other and are comfortable with the closeness.

Pulling away, leaning back, crossing your arms in front of you or resting your chin on your palm may come across that you're uncomfortable with him, putting up a barrier or bored.

3. TOUCH

A natural bond develops between two people who casually touch each other while they speak.

Not overtly sexual touch.

A gentle squeeze of his hand or shoulder, or a light pat on the knee will be reassuring, increasing his willingness to open up to you. Depending on his mood, rest your hand on him in a natural, comfortable way while he speaks.

Touch is not limited to your hands. Be spontaneous, uninhibited. Rest your legs across one of his. Stroke his feet with your toes. Sit on his lap. Or let him rest his head in your lap while you stroke his hair—or scalp. The possibilities are endless.

If you're in public, don't self-consciously fear what other people think. The world needs positive images of couples in love, so go right ahead.

Yet, you know your partner; some men just aren't comfortable with all that public 'touchy-feely' business. You'll help him to adjust, without him even realizing it, by doing it in small doses.

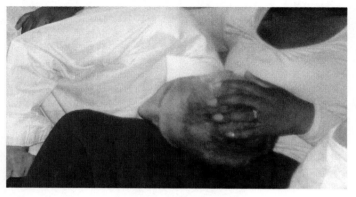

It was as Samson rested his head in Delilah's lap that he revealed the innermost secrets of his heart... *Interesting!*

For any man, too much touch can work against you and be distracting—unless the desire for distraction is mutual! But let's stay on track....

4. FOCUS

Remove all sources of distraction that are within your control, so he'll be certain that he has your 100% attention.

If you were reading, put your book down. Don't keep marking your place with your finger, waiting for him to stop talking so you can get back to your book. (Even if you really can't wait to get back to your book!)

Turn off your mobile phone.

Switch off the TV.

If you were working at a computer, turn around to face him. Don't just turn your head around, straining your neck. Swivel around completely in your chair. Let go of the mouse. Turn your back to the monitor.

If you have children, don't rush off to attend to a child who starts crying for your attention. Children seem to have built-in radars set to detect and disturb intimate encounters! Delay responding to your child as long as it's safe to do so. If you don't immediately rush to their need every time, they'll learn to solve their own problems. You'll actually be doing them a favour! Whatever you do, let your partner know that he is your priority—not just your children.

5. FEEDBACK

Feedback doesn't mean taking over the conversation!

It can be non-verbal, using eye contact, posture, touch, and focus. Make sure your body language sends the right messages.

Appropriate oral sounds can also enhance the bonding.

"Mmmmm."

"Umhm."

"Aaaah."

Simple sounds like these are quick and unobtrusive so they won't break his chain of thought but can be used to express agreement, disbelief, empathy, enthusiasm, excitement, fascination, intrigue, surprise, or sympathy.

"Oh my!"

"Yes."

"Good."

"Great!"

"Excellent!"

"Fantastic!"

"How absolutely interesting!"

"Really?"

"Wow!"

Short phrases like those above will also assure him that you're paying attention.

It also helps to briefly paraphrase what he's said or ask a few appropriate questions, to assure him that you're actively seeking to understand what he's saying. As with the other techniques, you must time your feedback to help and not hinder your partner's expression.

6. MIRRORING

Your partner will subconsciously feel at ease and speak more freely if you mimic or mirror what he does.

Smile when he smiles. If he furrows his brow, you do the same. For some people this happens naturally. It shows empathy. And really does help you to feel what he feels.

Obviously, you won't want to do this as an artificial, robotic imitation of your partner.

7. SENSUOUS LISTENING

Sensuous listening takes your experience to a whole new level.

Let me quickly note that there's a difference between *sensuous* and *sensual*.

Sensuality, which the scriptures are against, is the undue gratification of the bodily senses. It implies lewdness and carnality. But, when you're *sensuous*, you use all your senses to notice the simple pleasures of life and wholeheartedly embrace them with gratitude and enjoyment: the riotous colours of autumn leaves, the music of a flowing stream, the scent of pending summer rain, the texture of a wooden floor under bare feet, the taste of wild berries in the countryside....

When you listen to your partner sensuously, you notice the minute details about him, which other women overlook. You observe him closely with all your senses: sight, hearing, smell, touch, and taste. Not in an overpowering or obsessive way. And not for the sake of faultfinding or accusation. But simply for love of the man whom you're committed to for life.

You'll see the barely perceptible throb of the pulse near his eye. Or the tightness in his shoulders that yearns for a back massage.

You'll hear the changing intonations in his voice and use it to determine the emotions he's feeling. You'll know the unique scent of his body—with and without cologne. Perhaps you'll love to wear shirts he's worn when you're apart—if he doesn't mind—just to savour his body aroma in his absence.

You'll relish the firmness of his chest beneath as you touch him when you bid him goodbye. And you'll know the taste of his lips, and the skin on every part of his body that you're willing to explore when you spend time alone together....

But let's not go off on a tangent. Here's the final and most critical listening skill.

8. PUTTING YOUR HEART INTO IT

Merely applying techniques and following formulas is inadequate.

Simply adhering to a list of dos and don'ts leads to an empty, unfulfilling relationship.

So what's the 'crux' of listening to your partner? You've just got to want to do it from your heart.

Don't listen while secretly thinking that you have better things to do, hearing just enough words to masquerade a conversation. Don't listen halfheartedly, concentrating more on formulating your retort.

Don't impatiently insert your ideas of what he should say whenever he pauses to think of the right word. Don't cast hasty judgments, erect mental blocks, or snap out verbal disapproval or ridicule.

When you do this, how can you expect your partner to want to reveal the deep, inner thoughts of his heart?

Instead, your main motive should be to understand his point of view and empathize or feel with him.

This level of listening enables you to enter your partner's inner world and experience it with him. Your heart connects to his heart. Your spirit with his spirit. You'll experience with him the deep emotions that words alone are too clumsy to reveal. You'll discern even what he's *not* saying.

When you listen at this level, you'll give him your unconditional acceptance.[12]

Even if he painfully criticizes you, you won't lose your cool or try to defend yourself. Even if you think he's wrong, you acknowledge that his perception is real to him. Just allow him to express himself and give vent to his feelings. When you patiently hear him out, he'll reveal more and more of his heart to you, until you get to that tender, inner core where the root of the problem lies.

WHAT TO DO WITH THE 'SILENT TYPE'

If you're in a relationship with the so-called 'silent type', needling him to open up to you or complaining that he doesn't talk won't solve the problem.

He is silent because he associates more pain with talking than he does with bottling it all up.

If, for example, you ask, "What's bothering you?" and all you get out of him is a monosyllabic grunt, stay cool. Accept his grunt as a valid response. If you attack him

---

[12] Unconditional *acceptance* does not imply unconditional *agreement*. You won't necessarily agree with his perspective but you'll accept it, knowing that to him it is real and justifiable.

about his lack of response, you'll shut him up even more.

> **The 'silent types' are silent for a reason. They associate more pain with talking than with silence.**
> **Nagging them to open up to you will only shut them up more.**

Don't bombard him with probing questions. Be patient and respectful. Empathize non-verbally. Or just give him his space. Be sensitive to his needs. Give him whatever he wants. Do this consistently. Slowly but surely you'll re-build his trust, healing past hurts that led to his current silence. Bit by bit he'll re-learn to open up.

VERBAL CONSTIPATION

Have you ever been in a public toilet needing to let out all the stuff in your bowels?

Did you find yourself 'holding back', being too conscious of who may be hearing—or *smelling*—you? Do you remember the discomfort of that feeling? You don't want your partner to feel that he has to hold back for fear of your response to what he says.

Have you ever suffered from constipation? Do you remember the pain you've felt when you've desperately needed to release 'stuff' from your bowels, but for whatever reason, you couldn't? Can you remember the *euphoria* when you finally got to *'let it all out'*? That gives you an idea of the relief your partner feels when he can release his heart to you without inhibition.

PREDISPOSING FACTORS TO YOUR PARTNER'S VERBAL CONSTIPATION

- Repeated Interruptions.
- Jumping to conclusions.
- Responding with "Yes, but ... "
- Responding with "I told you so."
- Responding with a judgmental attitude.
- Responding to a complaint with a complaint.
- Hurrying him on while he is speaking.
- Arguing with him about the information that he dared to share with you.
- Assigning blame.
- Responding with sarcasm, insults, or criticism.
- Responding with a know-it-all attitude.
- Daydreaming while he speaks, preoccupied with your own thoughts.
- Concentrating on what you want to say next, while he's still speaking.
- Making an insensitive joke about what he's saying.
- Losing control of your emotions while he's speaking.
- Telling him insensitively what you'd do if you were he....
- Asking too many questions that seem important to you but may be irrelevant from his perspective, breaking his train of thought.
- Launching into a psycho-analysis of what he's said, as if you're his agony aunt.
- Betraying his confidence. Never let him hear someone else repeating what he revealed to you, for your ears only. The best way to do that is *never* to repeat it.

So, it's important to 'mind your ears'— master the art of listening to build intimacy with your partner.

But there's even more to 'minding your ears'!

You need to *be careful of the garbage that you listen to*. Because it will feed your mind. And you want to give your mind 'food' that will build your relationship and your perception of your partner. So be careful of the conversations that you entertain or the advice that you heed. Read on to the next chapter to find out more.

There's a friend of mine who was married to a tall, dark, handsome, and 'rotten rich' partner in a firm of chartered accountants. On the surface, it seemed that she had it all.

But deep down, she knew her relationship was in trouble. She felt that they were living like strangers in a huge, empty house.

He had not yet committed his life to Christ and she didn't approve of his lifestyle or his approach to business expansion, and wanted nothing to do with his business partners or parties. Her main involvement was to repeatedly confront him about the 'error of his way', using scriptures to back up her argument. He then began to respond to her with cold, calculated indifference.

With some encouragement, she took a different approach. One evening when he came home from work, she sat in his lap, stroked his head, and asked him about his day at work. *She just listened to his response while caressing him, without offering her usual judgment about the ethics of his business practices.*

She said he was so enamoured by her, that he spontaneously took her out to dinner at an exclusive restaurant—something he hadn't done with her for years. *(What else would you expect from an accountant? Ha!)* Anyway, humour aside, it was only when she stopped preaching at her husband and offered a loving, listening ear that she began to experience a measure of healing in her relationship.

SUMMARY

- Listening is a conscious choice that requires effort, concentration, and focus. It doesn't just happen automatically.

- Master the eight listening skills:
    - Eye contact
    - Posture
    - Touch
    - Focus
    - Feedback
    - Mirroring
    - Sensuous listening
    - Putting your heart into it.

- Talk less. Listen more. Love lots.

APPLICATION

- Monitor your feelings when you're in conversation with someone suffering from verbal diarrhoea. What patterns do you notice?

- Examine the list of predisposing factors to your partner's verbal constipation. How might your partner be feeling when in conversation with you? Be honest with yourself. What communication habits do you need to change?

CHAPTER SIX

CHOOSE YOUR COMPANY

Have you noticed a common conversation piece of many people today?

Complaining.

If it's not one thing, it's another.

Avoid them. Especially those who moan and groan about the faults of their partner.

Avoid those who're completely cynical about the idea of finding lasting intimacy because they've had—or know of—so many failed relationships.

There were just as many in Jesus's day who'd complain about him, plot his downfall, and criticize his actions and motives.

Like Mary, avoid that crowd.

They're toxic. They'll poison your thinking. And ultimately your relationship.

Remember Chapter 3? Choose your focus. Your focus creates your reality. So, stick with the crowd that chooses to focus on what's positive.

There are enough women around who are genuinely happy with their partners and fulfilled in their relationships. Hang around them. They're contagious!

Haven't met any? Well, begin a 'long-distance' association. Read their books. Listen to their CDs.

Have you ever heard it said that you can estimate the level of your income by averaging the income of your ten closest friends? Well, you can also determine the level of intimacy and fulfilment in your relationship by checking that of your ten closest friends.

It's an old but wise proverb that says, 'show me your company and I'll tell you who you are'.

Do you need to take a laxative? Wash out the 'stuff' you've been allowing in your system through the verbal feasts you've shared with your cynical friends?

Or does your circle of friends need a complete overhaul?

> **You can determine the level of intimacy and fulfilment in your relationship by checking the intimacy and fulfillment in the relationships of your ten closest friends.**

YOUR WORDS ARE 'SPIRIT'

You've already read about the power of your tongue in Chapter 4, but there's a bit more that needs to be said here.

When you complain about your partner to your female friends, *you're feeding thoughts into their minds about the negativity of your partner.* (By the way, if you're complaining about your partner to your male friends, you'll need to seriously question your wisdom!)

Anyway, when you get into the habit of complaining to others about your partner, this is what tends to happen. *Long after you've resolved those issues with your partner, those negative opinions remain alive in the minds of your friends.* Your friends will begin to respond differently to your partner and this will inevitably affect your relationship.

The negative words that you have spoken with your friends will only serve—in the spiritual realm—to pull you and your partner back down into that place of disagreement and un-fulfilment.

Your carelessly spoken negative words are like negative 'spirit' lurking in the atmosphere, seeking to be manifest in your relationship.

And they will continue to create—or give 'life'—to negative experiences between you and your partner.

If you have the kind of friends who don't respect confidentiality and will repeat your private business to others, that just adds momentum to the downfall of your relationship.

By the way, if you're single and you'd rather be in a relationship, when you complain to your friends that they're no good men around, you're creating that reality for yourself with your words. You're decreeing it over yourself as a self-fulfilling prophecy. Further, your friends are linking the power of their own thoughts and words with yours, when they agree with you that there are no good men around for you.

THE POWER OF AGREEMENT

The scriptures highlight the awesome power of unity and agreement in several instances. There's one that I'd like to point out.[13]

Whenever two or three people gather in agreement—like you and your friends agreeing over how terrible your partner is—what they agree on shall be done for them!

What are you unknowingly asking for, when you complain about your partner to your friends?

Choose friends who will not entertain any negative conversations with you about your partner ... or anyone else!

Instead, use the power of agreement to benefit your relationship.

Face reality.

Fact is, no matter whom you're with, you'll never see completely eye to eye.

So for some issues on which you disagree, just simply say to him, "Yes, darling." Or whatever endearing term you use. Say it sincerely not sarcastically!

Agree with him.

---

[13] It's found in **Matthew 18:19.** *Again I say unto you, That if two of you shall agree on earth as touching any thing that they shall ask, it shall be done for them of my Father which is in heaven.*

If he was expecting you to lambaste him with a strong argument of disagreement, you'll catch him completely off-guard. Without you having to say a single word, his very conscience will prompt him to reconsider the matter!

Try it! Let the *secrets of attraction* work for you.

Instead of agreeing with your cynical friends, why not agree with you partner for a change, and work the power of agreement to your advantage?

When you both stand in agreement, your influence increases exponentially.[14] And when you both align yourself in partnership with God, you are virtually invincible![15]

---

[14] **Deuteronomy 32:30** says: ... *one [shall] chase a thousand and two shall put ten thousand to flight.*

[15] **Ecclesiastes 4:9-12** reads: *Two are better than one; because they have a good reward for their labour. For if they fall, the one will lift up his fellow: but woe to him that is alone when he falleth; for he hath not another to help him up. Again, if two lie together, then they have heat: but how can one be warm alone? And if one prevail against him, two shall withstand him;* **and a threefold cord is not quickly broken.** (Emphasis added.)

As you may have noticed as I 'chit-chat' with you, my marriage is a 'threefold cord'—Robert, me, and God. I experience my greatest successes whenever I agree with and obey the directives of the 'third strand' in my relationship—even if, at times, I don't fully understand them.

In the years that I struggled with what I perceived to be my husband's *canine* sexual appetite *(ha!)*, I sought the company and counsel of older married women whom I trusted and thought would be able to give me good advice.

But I was very disappointed each time I asked for advice and I'd see their faces droop into lacklustre resignation as they considered their own situation.

"That's just how men are," they'd say. "Take your vitamins," another would remark. And I hated how often they told me that I had to be a *'dutiful wife'*. What would I do if sex became a mere duty? The sick joke would become a reality for me: *Marriage is not a word—it's a sentence—a life sentence!* It would be a lifelong test of endurance. And I did not intend to *endure* married life—I planned to *enjoy* it!

Thank God, I finally met a good woman about 10 years older than me who evidently enjoyed an incredibly fulfilling relationship with her husband—sexually and otherwise. She reminded me that my most powerful sex organ was my mind. She helped set my thinking straight. She helped me to overcome my old 'mental programming'. She recommended that I think about my husband amorously while I did all my demanding chores throughout the day, so that I'd be 'primed and ready' for his return.

We've been 'keeping company' ever since.

THREE UNRELENTING YET OVERLOOKED RELATIONSHIP KILLERS

We've already considered the devastating effect that *complaining* can have on your relationship. Here are two more relationship killers that too many women overlook: *correcting* and *criticizing*. It's the masses of women who don't know *the secrets of attraction* that resort to these tactics in their relationship.

If there's something that your partner is doing that you don't like or you don't approve of, don't give in to your baser instinct to complain, correct, or criticize.

You're not his mother. It's not your job to correct him. You may mean well, but the typical man won't receive it well. And though he may have a speck of matter in his eyes, what about the food stuck between your teeth?[16]

Complaining and criticizing are not solution-orientated. There is a better way.

---

[16] The principle is found in **Matthew 7:3**. *And why beholdest thou the mote that is in thy brother's eye, but considerest not the beam that is in thine own eye?*

EFFECTIVE CONFLICT RESOLUTION...
EVEN WHEN YOU'RE SEETHING MAD

First of all, while you're seething about the 'matter in his eyes' or whatever fault you're upset about, just remind yourself: that's not the best time to launch an 'attack'. Blasting anger and contempt doesn't result in lasting change.

Stop.

Calm down first.

Then, at the right moment, embrace him—physically, verbally, or otherwise—call him by name and say something positive and specific. *(I know: easier said than done! But it pays dividends...)*

Always precede whatever it is you have to say with a genuinely positive and affirming statement. Even better to 'sandwich' it: *start and end on a positive note.* You don't want to leave a bitter taste in his mouth when you're done with him.

Then, instead of attacking *who he is*, respectfully tell him how you feel about *what he does*. For example, don't say, *"You are so nasty and insensitive; the least you could do is clean up after yourself!"* Try instead: *"Whenever you shave and leave your hairs in the basin, I feel that you don't value me... "*

When you do it this way, you're not accusing, blaming, complaining, criticizing, or correcting; you're just airing how you feel.

Then, unlike what the masses of women do, instead of telling him how you want him to change, just *shut up*!

Any reasonable man will quickly offer a solution. You see, most women like to *talk* about problems; most men just want to *solve* them.

If nothing is forthcoming, consider asking, "What do you suggest we do, because I'm so happy in my relationship with you, that I don't want something as silly as that to get in the way?" You improvise. Choose suitably positive words that will work for both of you.

Then, once again, *shut up* and let him work things out with you.

Remember too, that you don't have to make an issue of every little, trivial disagreement.

Choose your battles.[17]

Commit some things to prayer or time. Let God and life orchestrate the solution for you.

---

[17] As the Jamaican proverb states, '*A nuh every fly weh pitch pan yu yu haffi shub weh*'. Transliteration: It is not every fly that perches on you that you need to shove away. In other words, *choose your battles!*

A MODEL FOR SUCCESSFULLY DEALING WITH DIFFERENCES

- *Calm* down first.

- Separate the *problem* from your *partner*. It's not your partner that's the problem; the problem is rather, an action, behaviour, or habit that your partner does, and how it affects you.

- Choose the *right moment*—make sure it's a good time for both you and your partner.

- Describe the *offending behaviour* respectfully and positively.

- State the *effect* the behaviour has on you.

- Be quiet and *listen* to his response.

- *Ask* for feedback, only if necessary.

- Commit to *start and end on a positive note*.

E.g., "When you do ... I feel .... What can we do about it?" In this way, both partners take responsibility for their feelings and behaviour patterns.

I've always chosen my inner circle of friends carefully. Only as a last resort—if I feel that we can't work things out by our own—do I confide in another person the serious challenges of my relationship. And it certainly would not be a complaint, but rather, seeking a solution.

Anyway, here's an experience of mine to illustrate that we don't have to 'fight every battle'.

We had our third child after an 8-year gap. It was therefore a new season of life requiring adjustments from all members of our family. It coincided with a time of increasing ministerial responsibility for both my husband and me.

There was a period in which we had several ministerial meetings to attend and I found it challenging to keep on top of all my responsibilities: 'wifing', mothering, breast-feeding, housekeeping plus ministry…. And the one I least enjoy suffered most. So I felt deeply uncomfortable with the state of my home.

Despite repeated conversations that we needed to slow down, my husband (who's been described as a *'race horse'*) just kept going at 'full speed'. It got so bad that I was ready to make an 'issue' of it. But I had an inner prompting from the Lord, to allow him to fight this battle for me. "Just leave it to me," he said.

A few weeks later, I was getting particularly impatient with God's timing, feeling that he needed my help to speed things up!

One morning we had an early meeting and had just enough time to ensure all our children were fed and dressed before dashing out (children in tow) to get to the meeting on time. I had to purse my lips to keep myself from complaining about it.

When we finally returned home that evening, we found a very worried-looking neighbour standing at our front door. In our haste, we'd left our front door wide open. And that's how he'd found it. He had just looked through our house to see if everything was OK. He said to Robert, "Looks like you've been *ransacked*."

We went inside to check through the house ourselves. It was just as we'd left it in the morning. Nothing was missing, but it was *terribly* untidy. I didn't have to say a word. Nor lift a finger. Robert 'bulldozed' through our home room by room and tidied it all himself.

I noticed over the next few weeks, his theme for our family devotions was 'slowing down' and 'taking care of our home'.

I was often tempted to get upset and say, *"I told you so!"* But I didn't yield—it's more important to preserve my relationship than to prove my point. *Selah.*

SUMMARY

- Show me your company and I'll tell you who you are.

- Choose friends who have found intimacy, trust, and mutual fulfilment in their own relationship and who will not entertain any negative conversations from you about your partner.

- Your negative conversations with the wrong kind of friends will perpetuate negativity in your relationship.

- You can resolve conflicts in your relationship by using this eight-point model:
    - Calm down first
    - Separate the problem from your partner
    - Choose the right moment
    - Respectfully and positively explain what offends you
    - Say how it makes you feel
    - Listen to his response
    - Ask for his input, if necessary
    - Start and end on a positive note.

APPLICATION

- Make a list of your ten closest friends.

- Are they in relationships?

- What are their relationships like? Would you want to emulate them?

- What three traits does your partner have that you find most offensive? Write them down. Think them through logically to help you overcome your heated emotions about them. How could you describe them to your partner and respectfully let him know how it affects you, *in a way that he can understand*. Write your answer down. It will help you to think more clearly, and make it easier for you to say it to him. At the right time, of course.

CHAPTER SEVEN

MONEY MATTERS

Did you realize that over two-thirds of broken relationships involve some kind of money worries?

Let's look at the third recorded encounter between Mary and Jesus as it sheds some light on handling money in our relationships.[18]

---

[18] You'll find it in **John 12:1-8**—*Then Jesus six days before the passover came to Bethany, where Lazarus was which had been dead, whom he raised from the dead. There they made him a supper; and Martha served: but Lazarus was one of them that sat at the table with him.*

Then took Mary a pound of ointment of spikenard, very costly, and anointed the feet of Jesus, and wiped his

Jesus sat to eat one of his last meals with his disciples before his crucifixion. Martha was the one serving the meal while Lazarus and others of his disciples were at the table with him.

Without warning, Mary came along anointing Jesus's feet with her very costly and exquisite spikenard oil. Then she wiped his anointed feet with her hair.

Mary was so intent on ministering to her master that she really didn't care what the others thought of her overtly physical expression.

The setting was particularly intimate, in the physical sense, as in their day, they wouldn't be sitting upright at a table to eat, but rather reclining with a pillow or cushion.

Mary continued her doting on Jesus and soon the whole house was filled with the fragrance of her oil.

---

feet with her hair: and the house was filled with the odour of the ointment.

Then saith one of his disciples, Judas Iscariot, Simon's son, which should betray him, Why was not this ointment sold for three hundred pence, and given to the poor?

This he said, not that he cared for the poor; but because he was a thief, and had the bag, and bare what was put therein.

Then said Jesus, Let her alone: against the day of my burying hath she kept this.

For the poor always ye have with you; but me ye have not always.

www.repositionyourlife.com

Some of the disciples were thinking, "What an absolute waste of money!" You see, in order to buy that quantity of spikenard oil, some of them would've had to spend a whole year's wages.

Finally, Judas couldn't take it anymore and he enquired, "Why wasn't this ointment sold and the money used for something worthwhile, like feeding the poor?"

Does this sound like any of the arguments that you and your partner have about how money is spent?

Jesus responded to Judas—like he previously did with Martha—hastening to Mary's defence.

Mary didn't care what others thought as she lavishly doted on Jesus.

"Let Mary alone," he said. "She's done this in preparation for my burial."

Then he made another enlightening statement, "You'll always have the poor with you, but you won't always have me with you."

☙☙☙☙☙❧❧❧❧

What secret can we learn from this encounter?

Mary realized that she'd always have the challenge of feeding the poor—just like you'll always have the challenge of paying the bills, buying the grocery, balancing the budget ... *but you won't always have the chance to spend lavishly on an intimate encounter with your partner—especially if he's going to die young, like Jesus did.*

Judas's statement could've left Jesus feeling under-valued and unimportant. Judas was prioritizing the poor over the Christ.

How often do you prioritize dealing with daily demands over building your relationship with your partner?

Unlike Judas (and the masses of women who do not know *the secrets of attraction*) Mary did not 'pinch pennies' in her dealings with Jesus. She planned a very expensive and intimate encounter to honour him!

Like Mary, do plan intimate encounters with your partner that are not ordinary, run-of-the-mill, or mundane. And they don't always have to be expensive.

What about a foot-massage after a hard day of work? How about a hot, deep, oil-scented bath (for two?) before bed-time?

やのやのやのやのやのやのやのやのや

For most people, how money is handled stems from deep, emotional issues that started in their childhood. So money often triggers major relationship disagreements.

This is especially true when either you or your partner has an 'unhealthy' relationship with money. Unhealthy approaches to handling money result in impulsive buying, hoarding and stinginess, gambling, avoidance of any thing to do with money (including simple things like paying regular bills), unawareness of your full income potential and opportunities, inability to live within a budget, and debt.

If your or your partner's attitudes toward money concern you, do consider how you may be contributing to it. For example, if he's a spendthrift, is it that he's trying to compensate for your own stinginess? Are you 'attracting' his spending habits by your extreme stinginess?

You'll need to aim for harmony in your handling of money by being open and honest with yourself and your partner, using the strategies of Chapters 4, 5, and 6.

Be prepared. It may not be easy. It may be emotionally draining. And you may discover aspects of yourself and your partner that have been buried for years. But do it right, and the resulting harmony will be worth it.

శ్రీ శ్రీ శ్రీ శ్రీ శ్రీ శ్రీ శ్రీ శ్రీ

There's yet another lesson to be learned from this encounter between Mary and Jesus. One that will virtually guarantee lasting intimacy in your relationship, in all the ups and downs of life. Read on to Chapter 8 to find out.

SUMMARY

- Like one cosmetic manufacturer often reminds you—*you're worth it!* And so is your partner. Treat him royally.

APPLICATION

- Monitor your thoughts and inner conversations about money.

- How do you feel it should be managed?

- How does that differ from how your partner feels?

- Do you have a budget?

- To what extent do relationship-building activities appear in your budget?

- Use the techniques of Chapters 4, 5, and 6 to have honest, open discussions about money, and to forge a way forward. Get formal help if you need it.[19]

---

[19] Excellent advice and (free) practical solutions can be obtained in the UK from national charities such as:
- Consumer Credit Counselling Service (www.cccs.co.uk), and
- Payplan (www.payplan.com).

CHAPTER EIGHT

STAY IN SYNC

Are you in touch with the changing seasons of your partner's life? Are you aware of his life dream? His frustrations? His fears? In what way do you seek to support and reassure him?

Up to six days before his approaching death, Jesus's disciples were *clueless* as to the significance of his life and his impending sacrificial death. Don't let that happen between you and your partner.

Mary, on the other hand, was tuned in.

We've read how she anointed Jesus feet with the costly spikenard oil—worth a year's wages—while he was reclining to eat a meal that Martha served, the house being filled with the fragrance of the oil.

When Judas challenged her actions, Jesus rose to Mary's defence, noting that she had done it for his burial. In Jesus's culture, dead bodies were anointed before being buried.

How was Mary so in-tune with what was happening in Jesus's life, while others appeared so out-of-touch?

Having developed the habit of observing him closely: his words, his moods, his actions, Mary had a seemingly intuitive ability to keep pace with the seasons of Jesus's life. She noticed when his focus was no longer feeding bread to the five thousand but rather offering himself up as the living bread.

Do you realize that in your partner's life, there'll be a season for frivolity and fun, but also a season for sobriety and solitude?

Be careful not to think that your partner is set in a mould, pigeonholed, and unchanging. He's growing and changing, just like—I hope—you are.

Stay in tune with your partner.

Don't allow yourselves to grow apart over the years.

Observe when his focus shifts from providing for the short-term needs of his family to making a long-term impact on the world.

Keep pace with him. *Don't remain a girl when he has become a man.*

❧❧❧❧❦❦❦❦

What's more, just like the fragrance of Mary's oil filled the house, so too will your unswerving support to your partner change the atmosphere of your home.

There is unprecedented power in your partnership! When you uninhibitedly commit to oneness with your partner, together you will release a unique fragrance that will change your home, your environment, and your world!

At least once a year Robert and I organize time away from all our children and daily routines to update our 'dream journals'. It benefits us both as individuals and as a couple.

We discuss in detail and write out what exactly is our dream for our relationship and the other important areas of our life. It allows us to stay in touch with ourselves and with each other. A few years ago, we did it a bit differently and had a most uncanny experience.

We went to an open field and had each other take turns at closing our eyes and describing in all sensory details (textures, colours, sounds, scents, etc) just what it is that we each dreamed for, while the other listened and took notes.

While I sat and listened to Robert, his dream became so real to me that it was as if I had literally stepped inside his mind and experienced it with him!

It was so 'mind-blowingly' exciting that I couldn't contain myself! Before he could describe it all, I told him what he was visualizing: the colour of his clothes, the material of his shoes, the kind of surface he was standing on, and even the aroma that he could smell. And it was all completely accurate.

When it was his turn to listen, he also described exactly the picture that was in my mind, down to the colour and texture of my outfit, my posture, where I was, and what the weather was like.

It could be that we know each other so well that we could predict each other's dreams in vivid detail. Or it could be that we found new levels of 'spiritual synchronization'. Whatever it was, it pays to apply this secret and 'stay in sync' with each other's lives.

www.repositionyourlife.com

SUMMARY

- Don't pigeonhole your partner, defining who he is for life.

- Be aware that he is growing and changing. Keep pace with him so that his need for you and your relationship doesn't become obsolete.

APPLICATION

- Observe your partner closely.

- What is it that makes him laugh? Cry? Angry? Passionate? What would you say is his life dream?

- How are you actively supporting that?

CHAPTER NINE

LOVE YOURSELF

Mary demonstrated the ultimate secret to intimacy and fulfilment in any relationship.

Until you tap into this secret, you'll *never* be truly fulfilled in your relationship ... or in life, for that matter.

It is simply: love yourself.

Until you learn to love yourself, you'll never truly be able to love another. It is only as you learn to accept yourself, forgive yourself, nurture yourself, and enjoy your own company, that you can do so effectively with another.

Selah. (Stop and think about it.)

Mary was evidently a confident, self-assured woman. *It must have taken a bit of spunk to anoint the feet of the reclining bachelor while he ate with his disciples.*

It must have taken a bit of spunk for Mary to anoint the feet of the reclining bachelor.

She openly and lavishly served her Lord and friend Jesus, not caring 'two hoots' about who was looking, what they were thinking, or what kind of gossip she'd generate.

She was decisive. She didn't second-guess herself, 'iffing and butting', wondering whether or not she should've spent her funds on the spikenard, or pining over the fact that she used it all in one night. She made her decision then acted on it.

While she allowed the luxury of splashing out on the spikenard, she didn't permit the luxury of nurturing a low self-esteem. She didn't harbour insecurity or waste energy by comparing herself with others, wondering if Martha cooked better or looked better than she did.

Rather she focused on her own strengths and what she had to offer. Mary was 'in-touch' with who she was. She accepted herself and was happy with that self.

She didn't come to the relationship empty, searching for a human crutch to carry her through life. She wasn't looking for someone to make her feel special, valued, or loved. She already knew she was special. She came to the relationship already full, having learned to love and value herself. And she was ready to share that self with another.

> **Don't come to your relationship empty, hoping for a human crutch to carry you through life.**

She had a life of her own independent of Jesus. Though he was the light of her life, she learned how to bask in the glow of that light even in his absence.

She gave him space to visit his other friends, to go fishing—or, if that was his thing, to watch football—to minister to the masses, and to fulfil his life purpose. *She didn't stifle him with her needs or overwhelm him with her expectations.*

She lived by *the secrets of attraction*, conducting a truly intimate and mutually fulfilling relationship: *love God and love your self to be truly empowered to love another.*

In essence, you need to apply *the secrets of attraction* to *yourself* first. Bring out the best in your own self.

Make the most of whom you are! Yes, you have your faults and nasty habits. Yes, there are areas of your life that you need to sort out. But remember that you are one-of-a-kind! You are created awesomely and wonderfully![20] You deserve forgiveness and room for growth. If you acknowledge that for yourself, first, it's far easier to see that for your partner.

Consider this: if you come to your relationship, feeling over-stretched, over-stressed, over-busy, critical, snappy, and exhausted, how do you expect that you'll treat your partner? Slow down. Take the time to do for yourself the *'one thing needed'*. Take time to enjoy your own company. Do what pleases you. Focus on your needs. Recharge your batteries. Only then can you effectively help to charge your partner's batteries.

Then, *take another look*. If you're tired of your life and everything just seems all messed up, are you inadvertently choosing to focus on your own dirt rather than the diamond? You'll experience increasingly

---

[20] **Psalm 139:14** reads ...*I am fearfully and wonderfully made: marvellous are thy works; and that my soul knoweth right well.*

more of what you focus on. Change your focus. Choose to savour more of the fulfilment rather than repeatedly rehearsing the frustration. It will soon become a habit for you to focus on the strengths of your partner.

How do you talk about yourself? What's the 'inner conversation' in your head like? Are you constantly putting yourself down? If you do, it will be far easier for you to keep putting your partner down. *Mind your mouth.* Get that negative energy out of your head. Begin to change your conversation toward yourself, first. Affirm yourself. Reward yourself. Congratulate yourself. It will then become far easier for you to do so with your partner.

Take the time to observe yourself closely. To reflect. To value your own opinion. *To* be your own 'listening ear'. *Mind your ears.* It will then become 'second nature' for you to listen to your partner.

Don't keep company with those who will put you (or anyone else!) down. *Choose your company*—develop a positive inner circle of friends whose life purpose is to speak life and to build you and everyone up.

Money matters. Money is a measure of your value. So every now and then make a date and pamper yourself. Very soon, you'll want to include your partner—who is an extension of you—in some of these lavish pampering sessions.

Stay in sync with your self. Realize that you're allowed to grow and change. Don't trap yourself in your 'history'. It's fine for the beliefs, values, and lifestyle that you held dear in your twenties to be in need of an upgrade when you hit your forties. Don't assume that you'll remain in a predictable mould for the rest of your life. When you do this for yourself, you'll more readily do it for your partner.

And finally, *love yourself.* Acknowledge that you are the unique creation of an Almighty God who loves you with an unconditional love. If God can love you so— even with all your faults—there may just be something in you that makes it worthwhile for you to love yourself!

The ultimate secret to loving your partner and finding lasting intimacy and fulfilment with him is to first *love God, love yourself, and then love him as you love yourself.*

There was a time in my life in which I was heavily involved in several areas of ministry, raising a young family, and coordinating several secular projects.

I survived on little or no sleep and took little or no time to nurture, rest, or rejuvenate myself. Eventually, I was burnt out and dried up.

I found little pleasure in ministry. I wished I'd never taken on the projects that I coordinated. And my impatience toward my tantrum-throwing toddler was exceeded only by my repulsion toward my husband. In my drained state, they both seemed demanding and self-centred!

I knew I loved Robert—or rather, had a 'duty' to love him based on my Christian faith—but I definitely didn't 'feel' the love. It felt like he was just one of the many who *wanted a piece of me*'.

The more burnt out I got, the less efficient I became—at work, at home, and in ministry—until I felt that I was pleasing neither man, children, self, nor God. I felt used and unappreciated, and like Elijah in the scriptures,[21] I felt it was time for the Lord to relieve me of my life.

And I actually prayed for him to do so. I'd never seriously consider taking my own life; I thought that I'd rather have the Lord do the 'dirty work' for me....

---

[21] Read **1 Kings 19:4**. ...*And he* [Elijah] *requested for himself that he might die; and said, It is enough; now, O LORD, take away my life; for I am not better than my fathers.*

Anyway, based on my distorted, over-worked, under-nourished, tear-stained perception, I saw myself as totally unfit to be a wife or mother, wondering why I ever thought to say 'I do' and why did I ever make the mistake of bringing children into the world.

My tears were really my 'meat' night and day. I continually defaced and berated myself in what seemed like a never-ending internal battle. I went as far as identifying (to myself) which more-deserving woman would 'replace' me as wife and mother after my demise...

Things grew incredibly worse because this was also a very demanding period in my husband's surgical career—long hours at work followed by significant mental energy and time devoted to ministry. So we were two incredibly busy people, heavily involved in ministry, but with insufficient time devoted to each other.

Then to make matters worse, on one of my projects there was a fellow who began 'buzzing' around me, apparently attempting to sample 'my honey' when my guard seemed to be down. Thank God for his grace in me, my commitment to live by his word, our commitment to openness and honesty as a couple, and my husband's unfailing love toward me in this difficult period. Despite the anger and the pain, we came through stronger than before.

But during that dark, difficult period of my life, I had to decide daily to live by *faith* and not by my *feelings*, or else, who knows what I'd have done?

www.repositionyourlife.com

I had to choose to remember God's clear word to me years back, when he directed me on the one to whom I should get married. I had to cling to the written promises of God, though from my distorted perception, they appeared to be lies. I kept repeating a verse from the scriptures to myself: *Let God be true and every man a liar!* Even when the lies seemed more credible than the God whom I'd served from my youth.

It was only when I applied this secret by slowing down to love, nurture, and appreciate myself that I overcame this dark era of my life.

It's paradoxical, but I needed to *slow down* in order to *speed up*. It's only when I slowed down that I accomplished more. Just like Elijah. He first needed to rest, then the Lord told him—via an angel—to get up and eat.[22]

I found my release only when I took the time consistently to rest and 'feed myself'. Both physically and spiritually. Even the Lord himself told his disciples to stop and rest after he'd

---

[22] Read **1 Kings 19:5.** *And as he* [Elijah] *lay and slept under a juniper tree, behold, then an angel touched him, and said unto him, Arise and **eat**.* (Emphasis added.)

sent them out in twos to minister.[23]

When you consistently take time out to love and nurture yourself you'll accomplish far more, have more to offer to your relationship, and everyone is happier—especially you.

---

[23] Read **Mark 6:7, 30-31**. *And he [Jesus] called unto him the twelve, and began to send them forth by two and two; and gave them power over unclean spirits; ...And the apostles gathered themselves together unto Jesus, and told him all things, both what they had done, and what they had taught. And he said unto them, Come ye yourselves apart into a desert place, and **rest** a while: for there were many coming and going, and they had no **leisure** so much as to eat.* (Emphasis added.)

SUMMARY

- Love God and love yourself. Until you do, you'll never effectively love another.

APPLICATION

Work the secrets of attraction on yourself first:

- *Make the most of whom you are.*
- *One thing's needed*—take some time each day to do what you really enjoy, to do what pleases you, to remind yourself of how precious you are.
- *Take another look*—focus on your strengths.
- *Mind your mouth*—affirm yourself mentally and verbally.
- *Mind your ears*—become your own listening ear; observe yourself closely; value your own opinion.
- *Choose your company*—select an inner circle of friends and mentors who will build you (and others) up.
- *Money matters*—make sure your budget allows you to splash out on yourself every now and then.
- *Stay in sync*—acknowledge that you're free to grow and develop; be 'in touch' with the changing seasons of your life.
- *Love yourself* first, to empower yourself to truly love your partner.

EPILOGUE

THE 'S-WORD'

The ten-letter 'S-Word'—submission—is a requirement of Christian partnerships in marriage. Husbands are challenged to love their wives as Christ loves the church; wives in turn are charged to submit to their own husbands as the church submits to Christ's authority. [24] This is so even if you are a

---

[24] Read **Ephesians 5:22 and 25.** *Wives, submit yourselves unto your own husbands, as unto the Lord. Husbands, love your wives, even as Christ also loved the church, and gave himself for it...*

Christian wife who is married to an unbelieving husband.[25]

Whether you like it or not, this is God's model. It's the authority structure that he honours. The husband has the veto. And when you consider that your husband is (or ought to be) seeking to love you as Christ, then you'll be assured that he's making decisions with your wellbeing at heart.

Of course, like every good leader, a husband ought to discuss issues openly with his wife in order to come to a final decision. He may also 'delegate' aspects of decision-making to his wife. But 'the buck stops' with him. When you run your own planet, you may concoct some other model!

Yet, to many Christian women, 'submission' is like a 'swear word' because it's associated with a loss of identity, independence and self-determination. For many women, just the mention of the word leaves a bitter 'doormat'-taste in the mouth.

Let's therefore clarify what submission is not.

Submission does not mean that you become a dog or a doormat to your spouse.

---

[25] Read **1 Peter 3:1**. *Likewise, ye wives, be in subjection to your own husbands; that, if any obey not the word, they also may without the word be won by the conversation of the wives...*

Submission does not mean you 'rent out your brain'. It does not mean that you remain in a life-threatening or abusive relationship.

Submission does not mean you go along with another person in an illegal act.

Submission does not mean that you passively agree to do something or live in a manner that goes against the scriptures, your principles, or common sense.

WHAT DOES SUBMISSION REALLY MEAN?

You could say that submission simply means: 'I put my mission under'.

It means that you voluntarily limit what you'd do naturally to please yourself, and focus instead on benefiting and honouring your spouse.

If you, like me, love to study words, submission—as used in the scriptures—comes from what was originally a military term, meaning: to arrange troops in a military fashion under the command of a leader. In a non-military sense, it means a voluntary attitude of cooperating, respecting authority, assuming responsibility, and bearing a burden.

Incidentally, submission is not only the responsibility of a wife to her husband.

The scriptures also give a general instruction for *all Christian believers to submit to each other*.[26]

So there's really nothing to specifically dislike about the principle of submission—except when its true meaning is contorted and distorted—for it is so closely tied to the principle of love.

But the principle of loving submission goes against the natural grain of modern-day living. In today's world, the goal is to take care of your 'number one'. That is, your self. 'Me and my needs' are the number one priority.

However, when you truly love someone, you're not at all self-centred, self-willed, or selfish. Rather, your goal is to honour, respect, and support the life-mission of the other. You don't seek primarily to have your own way, but rather, you submit: you prioritize the needs of the other.[27]

---

[26] Read **Ephesians 5:21**. *Submitting yourselves one to another in the fear of God.*

[27] Read **1 Corinthians 13:4-8a**. *Charity suffereth long, and is kind; charity envieth not; charity vaunteth not itself, is not puffed up, Doth not behave itself unseemly, seeketh not her own, is not easily provoked, thinketh no evil; Rejoiceth not in iniquity, but rejoiceth in the truth; Beareth all things, believeth all things, hopeth all things, endureth all things. Charity never faileth ...*

SHOULD I REALLY SUBMIT TO A 'GOOD-FOR-NOTHING-BEAST' WHO HAS NO REGARD FOR ME?

You may be wondering, "So what do I do if my partner's 'good for nothing' and doesn't love me like Christ loves the church?"

Let me remind you of my previous caution: do not remain in a violent, abusive, life-threatening, or illegal arrangement, under the guise of submission.

But, to answer the question, I don't believe that there's *anyone* who is truly 'good for nothing'.

However, I do believe that some of us have been so scarred by life experiences that we may appear to be 'good for nothing'. But in the right environment, and with the right opportunities to heal, we *all* have virtues that are lovable and desirable.

And what better environment for you to bring out the best in your partner than one of consistent loving submission?

So many of us—and possibly your partner—are so unaccustomed to being *loved unconditionally* that we've grown insulated, un-trusting, callous, and even cynical, for the sake of self-preservation. Your ongoing acts of loving submission and kindness toward him—regardless of his behaviour toward you—won't go unnoticed forever.

You'll write a new paradigm for him. You'll help him to begin to love and trust again.

So don't give up if you do not see immediate improvement after your first attempts. The scriptures aren't mincing words when they say 'love suffers long'. Only you can decide how long you'll 'put up' with your partner's ways ... let's aim for life!

DON'T EMASCULATE YOUR HERO

We've already seen some of the basic differences between men and women: men's super-charged sex-drive, men's desire to be problem-solvers, and men's tendency to talk less. (According to statistics, women speak an average of 7,000 words per day; the typical man crams a whole day's worth of talking into only 2,000 words.) One of the basic desires of the typical man (apart from the freedom to be and do all of the above) is to feel that he can make his woman happy.

So even though there may still be issues for you both to work through, *'just chill'!* Give him some slack. Get a sense of humour. Be happy. Laugh out loud. You don't always have to be working on your relationship challenges all the time. Stop. Enjoy the moment. Don't emasculate your man. Sure, he (like you!) will make mistakes along the way, but give him a chance to take the lead. To be your hero.

SUMMARY

- Submission means that you voluntarily limit what you might do naturally in your relationship to please yourself, in order to benefit or honour your spouse.

- But it does not mean that you 'rent out your brain', and agree to do anything that's illegal, life threatening, foolish, or sinful.

- The husband as the ultimate head of the home, under God, is the authority structure that God designed and endorses—like it or not!

APPLICATION

- How do you respond to the scriptural instruction to submit?

- Why?

ACKNOWLEDGMENTS

This book was born several summers ago, as I watched my husband playing with our two sons in the garden. I had an inner prompting to share with others the basis of our 'strong relationship'. At the time, I was working with several couples who were facing serious challenges in their relationships, so I enthusiastically began to record my thoughts on the matter. That's when 'all hell broke loose' in my own life and marriage, forcing me to live by *The Secrets of Attraction* daily.

Deepest thanks to all of you who've provided love and support over the years. In particular, thank you Mom and Dad, and Daddy and Mama Reid—your combined 93 years of marriage have set an example for me. I'm also grateful to other couples whose relationships have molded my own: Sammy and Valerie Stewart, the Martins, John Mark and Alicia Bartlett, and Melvin and Yvonne Brooks.

Also, thank you MD Kelly for planting that early seed of possibility in me that I could be an author, about 20 years ago when we spoke in your office! Thank you John Stanko for nurturing that seed. And thanks to all the women who confided in me as they sought to improve their relationships.

Marcia Levine, thank you for 'provoking' Robert into sharing life-transforming insights. One such conversation led to the premise of this book. I overheard Robert saying to you: *Who is the woman that you need to become to attract in your life the man of your dreams?*

Thanks to all those who agreed to review the manuscript, including the Brookses, John Stanko, Marie Anderson, and Kevin Hutchinson.

To my children, Andrew, Peterjohn and Abigail, who endured hours of my tapping away at the keyboard and (unfortunately) snapping halfhearted responses while I sought to complete yet another chapter: thank you for your patience, forgiveness and uncanny ability to 'bounce back'.

And Robert, how can I adequately thank you? You've been my friend for over half my life. You know me like no one else does. Yet you've stuck with me! Perceiving me to be greater than I am, and 'drawing out of me' a woman whose value far exceeds rubies.

Lightning Source UK Ltd.
Milton Keynes UK
UKOW052111081112

201886UK00004B/8/P